The Answers:

A Parent's Guide to Discussing Racism with Children

Troya Bishop, M.Ed.

CONTENTS

1 Examine Your Assumptions   p. 8

2 Frame the Discussion   p. 22

3 Use Appropriate Vocabulary   p. 28

4 Be a Positive Role Model   p. 38

5 Embrace Diversity   p. 46

6 Develop Strong Self-Identity   p. 51

7 Embrace Family History   p. 63

8 Encourage Curiosity   p. 67

9 Commit to Move Forward   p. 77

10 Conclusion   p. 82

11 References   p. 87

In Memoriam of an Educator, Politician, Civil Rights Leader and American Icon:

Dr. Julian Bond

January 14, 1940 – August 15, 2015

"I tell young people to prepare themselves as best they can for a world that grows more challenging every day. Get the best education they can, and couple that education with real-life experience in social justice work." – Julian Bond

Troya Bishop, M.Ed.

CHAPTER 1
EXAMINE YOUR ASSUMPTIONS
ALLOW YOURSELF TO THINK & WRITE FREELY

This workbook is intended to be a learning companion and guide for the book, *The Answers: A Parent's Guide to Discussing Racism with Children.* The intent is to make sure that you as parents have "the race talk" with yourself first, before approaching the subject with your children, or anyone else. This workbook will help you do that. You must know what you think and why you hold the beliefs that you do. Identifying what has shaped your thoughts about the world around you and the people in it is also essential; this workbook will help you do that as well. Keeping an open mind is also essential in this process of growth and learning.

Open-mindedness is the tool that prevents habit and desire from making you unwilling or unable to reconsider your beliefs, and revise or abandon them if necessary (Hale, 2013). The primary value in open-mindedness lies in challenging the fanaticism that comes from a conviction that our views are absolutely certain (Hale, 2013). Critical thinking skills are also needed in this process of discovery and recollection.

The importance of critical thinking is also stressed, because you may find this conversation difficult to have, even with yourself. Although the emphasis is on critical thinking, be patient with yourself, and allow yourself plenty of time to think through these questions and write your answers down. Then you will be ready to have "the race talk" with your children and perhaps friends and family members, in the most appropriate, effective ways. Use the stories you gather as you complete this workbook to serve as the core material you will share with your child. In doing so, they will honor you as a parent/guardian and respect your willingness to be transparent and vulnerable.

As a person who specializes in teaching adults, I understand that the most effective way to do so is by using critical thinking (Brookfield, 2004). With that in mind, I developed this workbook to help you discover the beliefs and assumptions you have. As you progress in the book, hopefully, you will discover ways to progress into the person and parent you want your children to emulate, as they move through this diverse world.

Critical thinking focuses primarily on two types of assumptions: power assumptions and hegemonic assumptions (Brookfield, 2004). In general, an assumption is a guide to a belief entrenched in your point of view (Brookfield, 2004). Assumptions are the daily rules that determine how you make decisions, and all of your communications (i.e. verbal, nonverbal) are subject to a continuous set of assumptions. We make assumptions about the meaning behind the words that we and others use, about the meaning of certain gestures, expressions or pauses, or about how to respond to a comment. Assumptions inform our judgments about whether or not someone is telling the truth, or how to recognize when we are being manipulated (Brookfield, 2004).

Power assumptions influence how we view power and relationships in our lives. Power is the ability to directly exert influence on things or people (Morris, 2015). Power can be defined as a means or as an outcome. Therefore, power assumptions have an impact on how we make decisions based on who we believe has the power to make things happen. If we assume that we are supposed to have power based on our ethnicity, and we don't have it, that greatly hurts the psyche. If we assume that we are not supposed to have power, and we obtain power, we may abuse it.

What assumptions do you hold as it relates to your ethnic group and the power held by the group in which you identify?

_____

_____

_____

_____

_____

How much power do you believe your ethnic group has to promote or influence politics and

economics on the local level where you live?

_____

_____

_____

_____

_____

_____

How do you feel about the power the ethnic group you identify with has? Does it make you

feel happy, sad, guilty, angry, etc.? How do those feelings affect your decisions?

_____

_____

_____

_____

_____

_____

How does the way you feel about your power affect the way you treat people from other ethnic groups? Do you feel powerful or powerless?

_____

_____

_____

_____

_____

How do people from other ethnic groups perceive you (and your power), at first glance?

_____

_____

_____

_____

_____

What experiences with power have you had or witnessed from childhood to present, that have shaped your thoughts and feelings? Recall several of these experiences to share with your children. Include the lessons you learned from each situation and how each experience made you feel. If you need help jogging your memory, ask childhood friends, family members or colleagues what they remember. You may be surprised by what you can recall, and surprised by how the feelings from those situations resurface. Use the spaces below to recall your experiences.

Elementary School Experiences

_____

_____

_____

_____

_____

_____

_____

_____

_____

Middle School Experiences

_____

_____

_____

_____

_____

_____

High School Experiences

_____

_____

_____

_____

_____

_____

_____

Work Experiences

_____

_____

_____

_____

_____

_____

Other Experiences

_____

_____

_____

_____

_____

_____

Hegemonic assumptions influence how we embrace particular thoughts because we believe those thoughts are in our best interest. Hegemonic assumptions work against you in the long term, because they misinform your beliefs and your behavior (Brookfield, 2004). For example, a White middle-class person spends one afternoon every Christmas volunteering at an inner-city soup kitchen. Afterward, that person shares their "expertise" about underprivileged people (Thomas, 2015). The hegemonic assumption made is that there is a right to authority or knowledge of the experience of poverty, based on that one brief experience as a volunteer. The privileged volunteer is tempted to feel noble about the rare glimpse into another world and tempted to "teach" other people touching lessons about the poor unfortunate people they encountered during their volunteer experience (Thomas, 2015).

What assumptions do you have about African American people? Men, women, and children?

_____

_____

_____

_____

_____

What assumptions do you have about White people? Men, women, and children?

_____

_____

_____

_____

_____

What assumptions do you have about children? Your children? Your relatives' children? Your friends' children? Children of other people you do not know?

_____

_____

_____

_____

_____

How might the assumptions you hold effect how you perceive events reported every day on the news and in other media?

_____

_____

_____

_____

_____

_____

What are the best and worst attributes of the ethnic group you most closely identify with?

_____

_____

_____

_____

_____

_____

_____

How do the assumptions you hold affect the information you receive about other ethnic groups? Are you able to effectively and open-mindedly process new information?

_____

_____

_____

_____

_____

_____

How can you replace assumptions with a commitment to open-mindedness?

_____

_____

_____

_____

_____

_____

Why is it important to understand what your assumptions are before you talk to your children

about racism?

_____

_____

_____

_____

_____

_____

CONGRATULATIONS!

You have now uncovered your biases and your true feelings about power. You examined your assumptions and challenged your beliefs. You have recalled past experiences and now you are ready to share those discoveries with your child. Remember to BREATHE, BE HONEST, and ENJOY sharing and being vulnerable with the people you love most in this world.

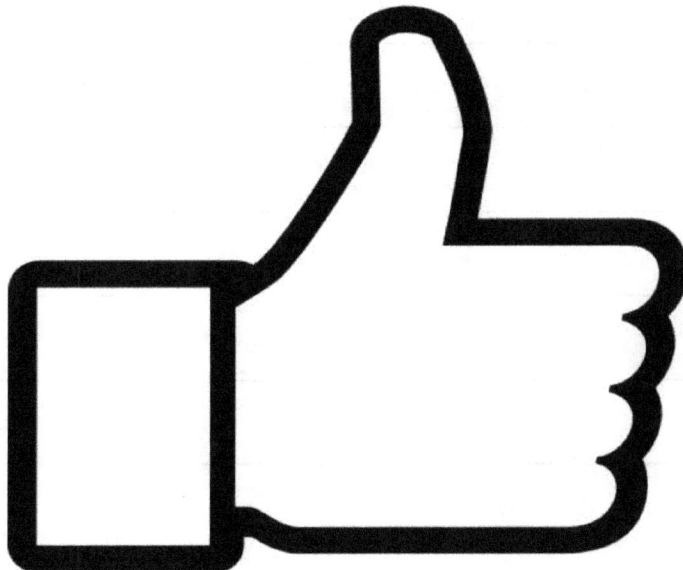

CHAPTER 2
FRAME THE DISCUSSION
HOW DO HUMANS RESPOND TO OPPRESSION?

We must begin with framing our discussion with the two components of racism: poverty and oppression. Oppressed and impoverished people have responded to oppression and poverty in ways that are consistent, regardless of ethnic group and geographical location. Use your favorite search engine to research historically oppressed ethnic groups in other countries.

How does your knowledge of the history of poverty and oppression affect how you perceive other ethnic groups?

_____

_____

_____

_____

_____

_____

On what continent and in which country do you think poverty and oppression looks most like it does here in the United States? What criteria are you using for your comparison?

_____

_____

_____

_____

_____

_____

How does a thorough understanding of the history of poverty and oppression throughout the world, affect your perception of African Americans' response to poverty and oppression?

_____

_____

_____

_____

_____

Since African American people have been free from legal slavery in America for approximately 150-152 years (arguably 1863-1865), which ethnic groups (historically and globally) are most similar to African Americans? Include a cultural (language, music, art, food, religion) comparison in your rationale.

_____

_____

_____

_____

_____

_____

What are other ways (perspective) to look at the plight and accomplishments of the African American ethnic group?

_____

_____

_____

_____

_____

_____

What is another way to look at the plight and accomplishments of the White American ethnic group?

_____

_____

_____

_____

_____

_____

_____

What alternative perspective of both groups resonates most with you? Why?

_____

_____

_____

_____

_____

_____

CONGRATULATIONS!

You have now uncovered your biases and your true feelings about oppression and poverty. You examined other ethnic groups that have survived poverty and oppression. You have recalled accomplishments of all Americans, and you are now ready to share those discoveries with your child. Remember to BREATHE, BE HONEST, and ENJOY sharing and being vulnerable with the people you love most in this world.

CHAPTER 3
USE APPROPRIATE VOCABULARY

One of the foremost experts on White privilege and racism in America is Tim Wise. He teaches that racism is both an idea and a system (Wise, 2015). It is the belief that certain people have characteristics or abilities, which make them superior to other groups of people. Racism is wielding power over another person or group of people (West, 2015). Therefore, people without power, cannot be racist.

Prior to reading the book, how did you define racism?

_____

_____

_____

_____

_____

_____

_____

In what ways do you agree/disagree with Tim Wise's explanation of racism being about power?

_____

_____

_____

_____

_____

What is the difference between prejudice and racism?

_____

_____

_____

_____

_____

_____

_____

_____

_____

Based on the definitions provided, what ethnic group(s) will you teach your children that you belong to? What contributions has your ethnic group made to American society and culture are you most proud of?

_____

_____

_____

_____

_____

_____

_____

_____

_____

_____

_____

_____

_____

_____

Micro-aggressions are forms of discrimination. There are three types of micro-aggressions (Sue et. al., 2009). The first is often referred to as a **micro assault**. A micro assault is a verbal or nonverbal behavior that is meant to hurt the intended victim through name calling or avoidant behavior (Speicher, 2014). Using racial slurs, or moving to avoid interacting with someone from a group different from your own, would fall into this category.

Think of a situation when you have used a micro assault and record it here. Share that situation with your child, and tell them what you would do differently now that you have a different understanding.

_____

_____

_____

_____

_____

_____

_____

_____

_____

_____

_____

_____

A micro insult is the second kind of micro-aggression. A **micro insult** is a type of discrimination that, includes any communication that expresses insensitivity and demeans an individual's ethnic heritage. (Speicher, 2014). Micro insults are subtle and are often unintentional, as compared to micro assault. For example, if someone is talking to a person of color and suggests they got their job, promotion, or admission into a university based on a quota system rather than merit; or by ignoring contributions of a person of color in the classroom or a group conversation (Speicher, 2014).

Think of a situation involving a micro insult. Write what you learned, and share that situation and lesson with your child (as appropriate for their age).

_____

_____

_____

_____

_____

_____

_____

_____

_____

_____

_____

The third type of micro-aggression is called a micro invalidation. A **micro invalidation** is any communication that minimizes, excludes, negates, or nullifies the psychological thoughts, feelings, or experiences of a person of color (Sue et. al., 2009). Suggesting that someone's experiences, interpretations, or feelings are invalid or are too sensitive, is a micro invalidation. Commenting to an African American that you, "don't see color," is invalidating that person's experiences as a person of color by suggesting that their ethnicity hasn't affected their life.

Reflect on a situation where you experienced a micro invalidation take place. Analyze your behavior, and consider how you responded and what you would do differently now that you have a new perspective. Share this experience with your child at an appropriate time.

_____

_____

_____

_____

_____

_____

_____

_____

_____

Institutional Discrimination is a web of institutional policies, structures, and practices that persistently generate benefits for certain ethnic groups, while creating disadvantages for historically marginalized populations (Lemley, 2014).

Why is it important to recognize institutional discrimination?

_____

_____

_____

_____

_____

_____

_____

_____

_____

_____

_____

_____

Dehumanization is a psychological process a person uses to justify the inhumane and unfair treatment of people of another ethnic group. Most often, this practice is used towards Black/African Americans, particularly towards African American Men. This process may be conscious or subconscious.

How has dehumanization of African Americans helped to shape what the media portrays most often about African Americans? How can this help to inform your conversation with your children?

_____

_____

_____

_____

_____

_____

_____

_____

_____

_____

_____

_____

The question I am asked the most, regarding the terms reviewed in Chapter 2 is about the term racism. Many parents (of various ethnic groups) will have an experience with their children and refer to their child's behavior as racist. Remember: racism is about power, and in most cases your child does not have power over other people and is not racist. They may be prejudiced and/or use discriminatory language and practices. That type of behavior must be addressed quickly and firmly, and you as the parent or primary caregiver must explain why their words or choices were wrong. You must also provide them with strong examples of how to make a better choice.

Consider this: If your child is consistently bombarded with negative images of African Americans and no positive images of African Americans, how can your child think any other outcome is possible? If your child is consistently bombarded with negative images of White people (especially images of older White people), how can they think any other outcome is possible? Regardless of your ethnic group, you must prepare your children to see **good** in all people, and in all ethnic groups, including those you identify with. That is the only way they will develop a healthy self-identity and a healthy understanding of other people in the world. I intentionally included the previous statement, because there are many people who see their own ethnic group unfavorably.

We all have biases. We must admit them, make concessions, correct our behavior, and require better behavior in ourselves and our children.

CONGRATULATIONS!

You have learned new vocabulary, and you can distinguish racism vs. discrimination. You examined past situations, and you are prepared to act if you see a racist or discriminatory act take place. You understand what dehumanization is, and refuse to use the word "colorblind." You see, accept, and celebrate differences in other people. Remember to BREATHE, BE HONEST, and ENJOY sharing and being vulnerable with the people you love most in this world.

CHAPTER 4
BE A POSITIVE ROLE MODEL
CHILDREN REPEAT WHAT THEY SEE AND HEAR

As established in *The Answers*, we know that children develop prejudice based on observing their parents' behavior. As such, creating an environment of allowing belittling other ethnic groups, and social behaviors related to those groups may encourage behavior most often referred to as "bullying," in American society. It is also discrimination. To avoid unwanted bullying and discriminatory behavior, parents should emphasize positive attributes of other ethnic groups, and demonstrate remorse and empathy when you say or do something inappropriate. With that in mind, as responsible parents, our goal is to find opportunities to be intentional with pointing out the good in other ethnic groups and people in general.

List some positive attributes about African American people as a whole.

_____

_____

_____

_____

_____

_____

List some positive African Americans in your community.

_____

_____

_____

List some positive attributes about White Americans as a whole.

_____

_____

_____

List some positive White Americans in your community.

_____

_____

_____

List some positive attributes about the ethnic group that you identify with. Or, if you identify as African American or White American, list positive attributes about any other ethnic group.

_____

_____

_____

_____

Admitting to our children that we have made a mistake is the foundation of teaching them to be responsible, and to own their mistakes. You can be a great example to your child 95% of the time, but children will catch you in the 5% that you mess up (Severe, 1997). Don't get defensive when your child catches you misspeaking or misbehaving. That's a valuable learning opportunity, and a perfect time to teach them about accepting responsibility for their behavior. I have had plenty of learning/teaching opportunities like this with my daughter Zoe.

I shared one of those stories in, *The Answers.* Think of a time when you have miss-spoken or said something regrettable in front of your child. Record that scenario below.

_____

_____

_____

_____

_____

_____

Now that you have a different understanding, and a renewed commitment to treating all people with dignity at all times, how would you handle that same situation, if you could do it all over again?

_____

_____

_____

Our biases can cause us to further injure victims of racism or discrimination. By refusing to acknowledge the anger and anxiety-provoking nature of racism, we add to the trauma and paranoia that results from the initial experience (Williams, 2015). This often results in victims of racism and discrimination feeling as if they are "going crazy." Chronic fear of and anger from experiences of racism often leads to hypervigilance and paranoia, which are contributing factors to post-traumatic stress disorder (PTSD) (Carter, 2007). As parents, we must recognize that trauma is real, and encourage our children to know with certainty that they must be empathetic to experiences other people have. Trauma is trauma, and we must be sensitive to it.

Have you ever wondered why it seems like African American people are often angry?

_____

Can you think of a situation/reason that an African American person may have experienced trauma?

_____

_____

_____

How do you think that a person who experiences trauma constantly, repeatedly, and systematically may behave?

_____

_____

_____

Do you think that person that experienced trauma received counseling or medication for that trauma?

_____

_____

_____

How do you think African American people have dealt with (or deal with) traumatic experiences?

_____

_____

_____

What may happen, if more African Americans are treated for PTSD?

_____

_____

_____

_____

_____

_____

_____

What are some ways that you or someone you know have experienced racism? If you are not African American/Black, feel free to use this opportunity to ask an African American person about racism they have experienced.

_____

_____

_____

_____

_____

_____

With these facts in mind, we must be committed to acknowledging the pain of other people and be as compassionate as possible. How can you show compassion to a person who may appear angry, while keeping your safety and the safety of your children in mind?

_____

_____

_____

_____

_____

_____

It is important that our children see us modeling empathy. Here is a list of a few scenarios you may be able to use to help your children empathize with others:

- Traveling in traffic or enduring a long family car trip? Ask your children to imagine how those who lived before them may have felt during travels in horse-driven carts and wagons? Or traveling shackled together on a slave ship? Or walking everywhere to get where they needed to go?

- See an abandoned car on the side of the road? Engage your child and their imagination, and ask them how the person may have felt when the car broke down? You may choose to go further into your child's emotional capacity to empathize by asking them to describe how the person may have felt when they tried to get their car towed, repaired, etc.

- Watching movies or your child's favorite show at home? It may be a good time to pause the movie/show and briefly discuss a situation that requires empathy on the part of one of the characters. Take advantage of the intimacy of your home to take a moment and discuss the characters decisions and try to predict how it will end.

Other Resources to Help Teach Empathy to Children:

ParentingScience.com

Parenting.com

TheBlackParent.com

Parents.com

MochaKidMagazine.com

CommonSenseMedia.org

RootsOfEmpathy.org

HandInHandParenting.org

CONGRATULATIONS!

You have now reflected on your parenting style, and considered ways you can teach empathy. You examined your assumptions about trauma and challenged your beliefs about ways to respond to people who may have suffered traumatic experiences. You have recalled past experiences, and now you are ready to share those discoveries with your child. Remember to BREATHE, BE HONEST, and ENJOY sharing and being vulnerable with the people you love most in this world.

CHAPTER 5
EMBRACE DIVERSITY
HIGHLIGHT THE POSITIVE IN OTHER ETHNIC GROUPS

As mentioned in *The Answers* book, by the time children start Kindergarten, they approve stereotypes and show prejudices based on ethnicity, age, attractiveness, disability status, and gender (Bigler & Wright, 2014). We should teach our kids early and intentionally about accepting other people, regardless of how they look. A great place to start is by trying new foods related to other cultures, and using that experience to explain differences.

The best place to begin is a place of familiarity. Maybe you have a relative or community member with a disability. Find positive attributes about that individual to discuss with your child. This would also be a good time to give an overall explanation about various types of disabilities and how you should react when you see someone who may have a physical disability. Also, consider using the ethnicity of public figures or celebrities to introduce the subject. Remember, we are NOT colorblind! We see color, we see differences, we respect and embrace the differences. We honor and love the differences.

Ask your child what celebrities they can name that they enjoy, whose ethnicity is different from yours.

_____

_____

_____

Now ask your child to list the things (adjectives) they like about that person.

_____

_____

_____

What attributes do you share with your children's favorite celebrities?

_____

_____

_____

_____

_____

_____

Depending on the people your child chose, this may be a great time to use a food or dish from another country to talk about that country, and the people from that country. What dishes can you prepare to give your children a cultural experience? What attributes of a culture do you share that you can highlight and discuss while you are preparing a meal?

_____

_____

_____

_____

_____

_____

You can also read books about children in other countries, and learn some simple words in a different language (Whittemore, 2009). What are some words or phrases from another language that you or your child may find interesting?

_____

_____

_____

_____

_____

Use your favorite search engine to find age appropriate books for your children. Using your local public library is also a great option for finding interesting stories about people from other ethnic groups. Talk to your child about the world and all the different people in it. Use a globe, allow your child to close their eyes, place their finger on the globe, and spin it! Where ever it stops, is where you will research! Research the people, the food, the politics, the animals, the music, the religions practiced, etc. Record your experience here:

_____

_____

_____

_____

_____

_____

_____

_____

_____

_____

_____

_____

CONGRATULATIONS!

You have now reflected on your parenting style, and considered ways you can embrace diversity. You considered different people from different cultures and walks of life, and have acknowledged differences as well as similarities you may share. You used your favorite search engine to discover other resources for teaching diversity and acceptance. Remember to BREATHE, BE HONEST, and ENJOY sharing and being vulnerable with the people you love most in this world.

CHAPTER 6
DEVELOP A STRONG SENSE OF SELF-IDENTITY
HOW DO YOU DEFINE YOURSELF & ETHNICITY?

Self-identity is the way a person defines her or himself, and how a person differentiates themselves from other people (De Cremer & Tyler, 2005). A person's ability to develop a clear definition of self is associated with the ability to: 1) effectively manage stress, 2) have balance between emotional connection and independence in intimate relationships, and 3) differentiate between their thoughts and feelings (Gushue et al., 2013).

How do you define yourself? It may be helpful to use your favorite search engine to assist you in finding the perfect terms to fit you.

_____

_____

_____

_____

_____

_____

How does your self-identity affect your ability to effectively manage stress?

_____

_____

_____

_____

_____

_____

_____

How does your self-identity effect your ability to have balance between emotional connection and independence in intimate relationships?

_____

_____

_____

_____

_____

_____

_____

How does your self-identity help you to differentiate between your thoughts and feelings?

_____

_____

_____

_____

_____

_____

Differentiated self-identity is seeing yourself in many different ways: ex., a mother, a wife, a child, a friend, a student, etc. An individual's ability to recognize a variety of ethnic and cultural perspectives (including complex ethnic and gender identity statuses) requires a differentiated self-identity (Gushue et al., 2013). This type of self-identity is open to multiple points of view and does not overreact to others people's assumptions and values. The construct of differentiation of self is understood as a form of psychological maturity in the areas of family and social relationships.

How may having a strong self-identity help you to accept others?

_____

_____

_____

_____

How may having an ability to differentiate your identity help you to accept others?

_____

_____

_____

_____

_____

_____

The definition of self-identity (that people develop and embrace for themselves), has huge implications for how they evaluate justice and respond to fairness-related events. For example, fairness communicates to people that they are valued and respected. In turn, the value a person places on the ethnic group they identify with also increases if they perceive that group is treated fairly (De Cremer, Tyler, & den Ouden, 2005; Olkkonen & Lipponen, 2006).

How may the historic and current treatment of African Americans people effect their self-identity?

_____

_____

_____

_____

_____

_____

Research indicates that people who have a more mature sense of ethnic identity have healthier and more developed psychological functioning (Buckley & Carter, 2005; Nghe & Mahalik, 2001). Put simply, if you can see yourself in several different ways, from several different perspectives, you are more likely to be able to accept people who are different from you.

Ethnic identity is how a person defines her or himself based on commonalities shared with other people. These commonalities include: physical appearance, language, customs, religion, history, nation/region of origin, ways of being, names, physical appearance, and/or genealogy or ancestry (Markus, 2008).

How may an unfavorable attitude toward your ethnic identity effect how you treat others?

_____

_____

_____

_____

_____

_____

Research also verifies that justice affects self-identity activation on an explicit and implicit level. It balances the effects of justice on trust, cooperation, and counterproductive behavior (Johnson & Lord, 2010). The construct of a person's self-identity is directly impacted by how justly they believe they have been treated, and is an indication of psychological maturity.

In today's social climate in America, how may the self-identity for African American people be effected by the perception of rampant injustice in education, housing, lending/banking, policing, mass incarceration, sentencing, etc.?

_____

_____

_____

_____

_____

_____

How might an African American person's beliefs about justice effect their differentiated identity?

_____

_____

_____

_____

_____

_____

As humans, there are certain undeniable scientific facts that transpire when we communicate. At the moment we make contact with other people, biochemical reactions are triggered at every level of our bodies (Glaser, 2014). Our heart responds in two ways — electrochemical and chemical. When we interact with others, we have a biochemical or neurochemical response to the interaction. We also receive electrical signals from others during that interaction. As our bodies read and process another person's energy (which we pick up within 10 feet of the person) the process of connecting or rejecting begins (Glaser, 2014).

Have you experienced an automatic, physiological (biochemical) reaction to someone? Describe the feeling that comes to mind.

_____

_____

_____

_____

_____

Have you experienced a biochemical reaction to a loved one? Family member? Old lover? High School classmate?

_____

_____

_____

_____

_____

_____

Have you experienced a biochemical reaction to a stranger? Someone you just met? Describe that person and that feeling.

_____

_____

_____

_____

_____

_____

Compare the differences in your reaction to someone you thought well of, and your reaction to someone you didn't know or trust? What was the same/different in your biochemical reaction?

_____

_____

_____

_____

_____

_____

_____

How may identifying yourself first as human (in your personal definition of self-identity) change the way you connect with other people?

_____

_____

_____

_____

_____

_____

How may it change your biochemical reaction to make people you don't know feel more comfortable/willing to get to know you?

_____

_____

_____

_____

_____

_____

_____

As Americans, most people would agree that the cultural aspects that identify America the most are the art forms of Rock-N-Roll, Jazz, R&B, and Hip Hop, along with the dance forms, vernacular, and styles of dress which accompany each art form.

With this in mind, how do you think learning about these art forms will affect the self-identity of African American youth and teenagers?

_____

_____

_____

_____

_____

_____

_____

Note: For more detailed information for developing self-identity for Black/African American children visit the websites and exquisite work of Dr. Na'im Akbar and Dr. Chike Akua. NaimAkbar.com and MyTeacherTransformation.com

CONGRATULATIONS!

You have defined your self-identity and differentiated your identity. You examined research regarding self-identity and justice. You have synthesized that data and made it relevant to your understanding of the plight of African American people. You will use your notes to teach your child about their identity. Remember to BREATHE, BE HONEST, and ENJOY sharing and being vulnerable with the people you love most in this world. Who's #1? YOU ARE!

CHAPTER 7
EMBRACE FAMILY HISTORY
ACCENTUATE THE POSITIVE

In each city across America, there are events that took place that shaped that community. Having a discussion about who your family is, and how they have shaped the community, city, county, or state where you reside can provide your children with a huge sense of pride and ownership, regarding moving the community forward.

There are many websites and companies that can help you accurately trace your family history. If possible, use those resources to find out more information about your lineage. Even if the information you have access to is limited, write about what you know about your family and what they contributed to your community. Share that with your child. Include the following in your research: Maternal/Paternal Grandparents and their children up to your child's generation; City/State/Country of origin; How they met; When they moved to other places; What motivated them; Various family occupations; Religious beliefs; Etc.

_____

_____

_____

_____

_____

_____

_____

_____

_____

_____

_____

_____

_____

_____

The influence of our family members on the way we "remember" a past that we have not lived through is a basic part of our **mnemonic socialization**; which is the way we learn to remember and interpret the past (Zerubavel, 1996). This socialization begins within the family, and we gradually apply or revise what we have learned as we venture out into the community and the world at large. With this in mind, we must find the positive things our family members accomplished; accomplishments of individual family members or accomplishments that are shared collectively.

Find the oldest member of your family, and take your child to visit and interview that family member. Ask that family member the questions on p. 71. Use the information you gather to positively shape your story and form your family plan on how you will continue to move your family forward.

_____

_____

_____

_____

_____

_____

_____

_____

_____

_____

_____

Please Note: I want to emphasize the need to tell the truth about the past, even if it is difficult. I also want to emphasize the need to find family members that contributed in a positive way to society. This will keep the perspective geared toward <u>healing and moving the family forward</u> with a new perspective and a commitment to a brighter future.

CONGRATULATIONS!

You have now reflected on your family history and considered ways you can continue to shape your identity. You considered the past contributions your family has made and have determined ways to make improvements in the future. You used your favorite search engine to discover other facts about your family, your culture, and your history. Remember to BREATHE, BE HONEST, and ENJOY sharing and being vulnerable with the people you love most in this world.

YOU ROCK!

CHAPTER 8
ENCOURAGE CURIOSITY
TEACH AND DEMONSTRATE CRITICAL THINKING

As established in *The Answers,* **Critical thinking** is a person's ability to consider data and decide how the information should be used based on accuracy (Bishop, 2016). To develop critical thinking skills, you must be curious, open-minded and willing to consider alternative ways of looking at problems and ways to solve those problems. You must also look at factors, and determine if one caused the other.

Are you a critical thinker? What evidence do you have that you are/ or are not?

_____

_____

_____

_____

_____

_____

_____

Kids are naturally inquisitive, so encouraging them to be curious and ask questions should not be difficult. As children grow into pre-adolescents and teenagers, their critical thinking skills will help them make good decisions when their parents are not around (Bishop, 2016). This is the goal for most parents.

To be good at thinking, children must believe that thinking is fun and *want* to be good at it. Good thinkers practice thinking just like they would practice a new dance or their favorite sport (Bishop, 2016). We must encourage our children to practice thinking, from an early age. Here are some ideas to encourage critical thinking and problem solving in your children:

Provide opportunities to play. It is during play that children test their thinking (Bright Horizons Family Solutions, 2016). Unfortunately, play time and recreational activities have been removed from the curriculum in most schools. As such, it is important for us as parents to make sure we create opportunities for play outside of school.

Providing space for playing, including time for outdoor or pretend play, can give your child unlimited opportunities to try something new and see the effect (Bright Horizons Family Solutions, 2016). Whether a child is dropping a spoon over and over again off the side of a high chair tray; rolling two marbles down a chute to see which marble is faster; seeing what happens when you dip chalk in water; or mixing cornstarch and water to make "goop" - all of these playful activities help a child develop critical thinking skills. You can encourage them to try it a different way than they tried it the first time. This informal process of testing how things work is crucial to developing critical thinking (Bright Horizons Family Solutions, 2016).

Help children view themselves as problem solvers and thinkers by asking open-ended questions. Rather than automatically giving answers to the questions they ask, help them think critically by asking questions in return: "What do you think? What ideas do you have?

What do you think is happening here?" Respect his or her responses whether you view them as correct or not. You could say, "That is interesting. Tell me why you think that." Use phrases like "I am interested to hear what you think about this." "How would you solve this problem?" "Where do you think we might get more information about this problem?"

Depending on the age of your child and your judgement of their maturity level, you may ask them some of the following questions and compare them with yours:

What do you think about how the United States repaid the African captives (slaves) for all of years of servitude and torture they endured?

_____

_____

_____

Tell me why you think that?

_____

_____

_____

Where do you think we may be able to get more information about how people from different countries have been compensated after being mistreated?

_____

_____

_____

Help children develop hypotheses. "If we do this, what do you think will happen?" "Let's predict what we think will happen next."

Encourage thinking in new and different ways. By allowing children to think differently, you're helping them hone their creative problem-solving skills. Ask questions like, "What other ideas could we try?" or encourage coming up with other options, "Let's think of all the possible solutions."

Support your child to research further information. You can help your children develop critical thinking skills by encouraging them to look for more information. Say, "Now how could we find out more? Your uncle knows a lot about this. Let's ask him? Or maybe we should search the internet?" All of those ways encourage critical thinking, curiosity, and problem-solving skills.

Young children can understand critical thinking, and will automatically apply it when they believe it benefits them. Consider how many times you have heard your child say, "that's not fair", or "that's not nice", or something of that nature. When children believe something is unfair, they know and are able to boldly articulate it. It is at times like this, that you can teach your child to use critical thinking. You can also teach them to think critically about the basics of human cruelties like slavery and bullying (Bishop, 2016).

As it relates to racism, and the race talk, a parent can use this scenario and ask follow-up questions:

Slavery happened about 150 years ago in this country. Holding people captive and making them work without paying them is unfair. You can use the follow-up questions:

Why do you think slavery was wrong?

_____

_____

_____

_____

How do you think you would feel if you were held captive and made to work for free?

_____

_____

_____

_____

What repayment do you think is fair for people who were a victim of slavery?

_____

_____

_____

_____

What consequence do you think is fair for people who were slave owners?

_____

_____

_____

_____

As parents, we can explain to our children that slavery ended, because many people thought it was wrong and worked to change it. You can then extend the conversation and encourage critical thinking by asking:

Have you ever seen someone being treated unfairly?

_____

_____

What did you do to change the situation?

_____

_____

What do you think you could have done differently?

_____

_____

Again, it is important to emphasize that no ethnic group is all bad or all good. Asking your child questions about the difference in how "good people" and "bad people" behave is also good place to teach critical thinking. Consider this example, and expound on it with your children:

In the United States, some White people were slave owners, but some White people also worked against slavery. Black people were enslaved, but many resisted the mistreatment and abuse by running away and helping others escape.

Offering your children examples of different perspectives of any issue promotes critical thinking and encourages them to embrace diversity. It also helps them to become problem solvers, and enhances their ability to appreciate other perspectives. Unfortunately, our own biases and prejudices often keep us as parents from presenting alternate perspectives.

As parents, we want to encourage our children to think for themselves, and groom them to be leaders and to avoid peer pressure. We want them to have the skills to effectively analyze, listen, and interpret information that will affect their lives and the lives of those around them (Garland, 2014). After the remembering and understanding levels of Bloom's taxonomy, the next four levels are higher levels of thinking that we want to encourage our children to develop.

The last four stages are: applying, analyzing, evaluating and creating. In the applying stage, children are asked to use a concept in a new situation and apply what they know. Or, a parent may also ask why something is significant, or ask their child to predict what will happen next in a given situation (Bishop, 2016).

Depending on the age and maturity level of your children, this may be a great place to extend the conversation of slavery by evaluating the effects of slavery on the Black family and analyzing the repayment to descendants of slaves.

Slavery ended about 150 years ago (or two 75-year-old grandmothers ago). The Constitution promised each slave 40 acres and a mule so they could work and feed their families. However, most African Americans never got it, and they continued to suffer in extreme poverty and oppression. Should the remaining descendants of slaves be given something to compensate them for slavery?

Should they be given tax breaks? Land? Student Loan forgiveness?

_____

_____

_____

As previously mentioned, this is a good time and place in working with your child to model empathy and compassion. After asking several higher level Bloom's Taxonomy questions, during various conversations, you will get a feel of your child's ability to think critically. Be patient and give your child extra time to respond. If your child is not used to higher level questioning or using their brain for this type of thinking, it may take some time for them to process the information and be able to respond. With practice, higher-level questioning will become easier for you and your child.

CONGRATULATIONS!

You have now reflected on your use of critical thinking. You have considered different ways to model critical thinking to your children. You learned different strategies to help them become more savvy critical thinkers. You used your favorite search engine to help your children discover how to connect the dots between how things happen in history and why. Remember to BREATHE, BE HONEST, and ENJOY sharing and being vulnerable with the people you love most in this world.

Good job!

CHAPTER 9
COMMIT TO MOVE FORWARD
WHAT DO I DO WITH THIS NEW PERSPECTIVE?

Now that you and your children have: examined your assumptions, framed the discussion on racism, embraced who you are as a family unit and piqued your collective curiosity, it is time to connect the dots, and move forward with what you have learned.

There are two crucial steps that are necessary to commit to in the process of moving forward. The first is simple, but it can be difficult. **Talk about the reality of racism when the opportunity presents itself.** Being able to recognize racism, and empathize with those who have historically suffered the trauma and effects of racism is crucial to moving forward (Bishop, 2016).

It is also important to acknowledge that due to the institutional nature of racism, most African American people, still feel the effects of racism on a regular (daily) basis. Admit this truth as often as possible, in as many ways as possible. There are millions still living in denial about the ugliness and pain of racism. Your willingness to speak the truth, even when it is not popular is vital to the continued growth and development of America.

Speaking the truth at all times, includes being willing to share your views of the truth on social media, at church, at family gatherings, at work, and any other social setting. Remember, racism is a disorder of relationships (Bishop, 2016). As the relationally-well individual in social situations, it is imperative that your powerful voice is heard.

The problem in our very individualistic, American society is the plethora of messages that reinforce the narcissistic notion that, "it's all about you" (Plante, 2013). The willingness to discuss racism may be uncomfortable, and it may challenge others to be uncomfortable as well. However, it is important and very necessary.

The federal government has a critical role to play in addressing the issue of ethnic disparities in mental health status and mental health care by supporting legislation and regulations that will improve the health and well-being of minorities. (APA, 2015). Further, the federal government has a responsibility in particular to African American people to right the wrongs of slavery and racism. As such, the second commitment in moving forward is also simple, yet difficult. **Talk about the need for reparations for African-American people to peers and elected officials**.

"Two hundred fifty years of slavery. Ninety years of Jim Crow. Sixty years of separate but equal. Thirty-five years of racist housing policies. Until we reckon with our compounding moral debts, America will never be whole" (Coates, 2014). We are not the first to be summoned to such a challenge as reparations.

In 1952, when West Germany began the process of making amends for the Holocaust, it did so under conditions that Americans can learn from (Coates, 2014). Initially, there was violent resistance to the idea of reparations for Jews in Germany and very few Germans believed that Jews were entitled to anything. Only 5% of West Germans surveyed reported feeling guilty about the Holocaust, and only 29% believed that Jews were owed restitution from the German people (Coates, 2014).

Tony Judt wrote in his book, *Postwar*, that the rest of the Germans were divided between: those who thought that only people "who really committed something" were responsible (and should pay), and those who thought "that the Jews themselves were partly responsible" for what happened to them during the Holocaust (2005). After a lot of violence and further bloodshed, Jews were finally given reparations, and their bloody history was restored to the financial and historical fabric of German society. As Americans, we must be unwilling to repeat German history, and to learn from the mistakes others have made in the past. Reparations for African Americans can be easily implemented in many different ways. I will suggest a few.

One simple step in the right direction is free college tuition for all African Americans. Another is student loan forgiveness for all African American people. Those measures are simple to implement. Waving federal taxes for all people who identify as Black American or African American is also a relatively simple way to repay the descendants of slaves for building the robust economy in America. Take the time to discuss with your peers and elected officials other ways that reparations can be implemented in your city or state. Of course, we all have power and influence on some level, and if yours has a federal reach, by all means use it.

What are some ways that reparations have been implemented in other countries? Use your favorite search engine to discover reparations in other nations and list them here.

_____

_____

_____

_____

_____

_____

Who has power or influence that you can set up a meeting with to discuss reparations?

_____

_____

_____

_____

_____

_____

Our job as people of conscience, is to begin that conversation with our peers and elected officials. Surely if we are wronged in medical malpractice or a car accident, we will want and expect financial compensation. Reparations for African Americans is past due, and absolutely necessary.

CONGRATULATIONS!

You have now reflected on your commitment to talk about racism and reparations. You have considered different ways to model a discussion about reparations and racism in a constructive way. You used your favorite search engine to help your children discover how people historically have been repaid for injustices they have suffered. You have brainstormed some ideas on how African Americans can receive reparations. Remember to BREATHE, BE HONEST, and ENJOY sharing and being vulnerable with the people you love most in this world.

CHAPTER 10
CONCLUSION
STAY COMMITTED TO THE MOVEMENT

The consistent lack of understanding in the United States about how people respond to poverty and oppression globally has contributed to the overall dehumanization of Black and Brown people around the world, especially African Americans. Parents of all ethnic backgrounds must be intentional with teaching their children about the humanity of African-American people, to ensure that they perceive and value Black and Brown people as human beings. The use of appropriate vocabulary is absolutely necessary when discussing racism with children. Parents should also be more aware and intentional with the behavior they are modeling because your children are watching and will duplicate the behavior parents and guardians display.

Racism-related experiences can range from frequent micro-aggressions to blatant hate crimes and physical assault (Williams, 2015). Micro-aggressions are pervasive acts of racism; they can be vague insults or non-verbal exchanges, such as a scowl or refusal to sit next to a Black person in a meeting or on public transportation. During micro-aggressions, the victim loses key mental and emotional capacity trying to understand the intention of the perpetrator (Williams, 2015). Keeping in mind the institutional and often direct and interpersonal nature of racism, all society members must acknowledge that these events happen frequently, making it difficult for many African-Americans to mentally and emotionally manage the volume of racial stressors. We as guardians, parents and community members should demonstrate a sympathetic response to pain and hurt, whether we encounter it in the media or in person.

Our behavior must model and reflect genuine concern, and not dismissiveness. We must encourage our children and others to see the beauty and differences in others. If you choose to be colorblind and promote colorblindness in your children, you teach them not to appreciate the uniqueness of people who are different from them. We are different in appearance, and being different is great. We must remind our children that there is only one race: the human race.

Zig Ziglar, an American author, salesman, and motivational speaker reminds us in his book, *The Answer to Racism*, that even the Bible does not use the word race in referring to people. Instead, it describes all human beings as being of "one blood" in Acts 17:26 (Ziglar, 2015). This further emphasizes that we are all related, and all humans are descendants of the first man and woman. With this in mind, we must make a collective effort to walk in unity.

Dr. Tony Evans, the first African-American to earn a doctoral degree from Dallas Theological Seminary, reminds us that unity does not equal sameness (1995). People from different cultures, religions, and ethnic groups can have unity, without being the same or believing the same things. Unity is a requirement for healthy families and communities. Unity is also a requirement for a healthy marriage, although the husband and wife are different physically, and in their personality and temperament (Evans, 1995), God still requires them to walk in unity. Unity requires oneness of purpose. That means all parties are willing to move forward in a positive direction for the common good of all involved (Evans, 1995). Of course, unity is simple, but not easy. Unwillingness to consider the other person and walk in unity is the reason behind the hostility in our culture, and the reason for the increasing amounts of failed marriages. However, when people refuse to cooperate with efforts of progress and unity, we must hold them accountable (Evans, 1995).

All community members, parents and those without children should speak up and speak out when they see wrongdoing. The visible leadership of the Christian church cannot condone public rejection of people who are different (Evans, 1995). There is no more time for us to sit by passively and wait for people to change. People must be willing to learn and remain committed to the process of life-long learning; that cannot be done without the knowledge that they will be held accountable for how they treat other members of God's family (Evans, 1995).

One of the most poignant teachings regarding truth, culture, and unity is in John 4, when Jesus Christ encountered a woman from Samaria. This story provides outstanding principles for people of different faiths and different ethnic backgrounds that are needed to establish unity (Evans, 1995). Ultimately, we as parents must be careful of what we say and the way we say it.

Words are powerful. We must be sure to model appropriate vocabulary and to use words in their proper context. Our children are watching, and they will see and say everything we model. World-renowned poet, actress, singer, and five-time Grammy winner, Dr. Maya Angelou, stresses that, "Words are 'things.' You must be careful about the words you use, or the words you allow to be used in your house... Words are things. You must be careful. Careful about calling people out of their names. Using racial pejoratives, and sexual pejoratives, and all of that ignorance. Don't do that. Someday we will be able to measure the power of words. I think they are things. I think they get on your wall. They get in your wallpaper, and in your rugs. They get in your upholstery and your clothes, and finally, they get into you." (Angelou, 2011). As we protect what goes into our minds and out of our mouths, we must be careful to behave as we want our children to behave: as compassionate, loving, fair people.

As we want understanding and empathy from other people, we must find it in ourselves to give it to other people, all people. Dr. Angelou also explained, "I have had so many rainbows in my clouds, and I've had a lot of clouds. But I have had so many rainbows…The thing to do it seems to me is to prepare yourself so that you can be a rainbow in somebody else's cloud. Somebody who may not look like you, or may not call God the same name you call God, if they call God at all… They may not eat the same dishes prepared the way you do. They may not dance your dances, or speak your language, but be a blessing to somebody." (Angelou, 2011). Taking this step is the key to embracing diversity.

Changing the way you think, and being willing to make decisions to have a lifestyle which includes people from other ethnic groups is essential. Again, our children will listen to us and follow us when they know we are authentic. According to Dr. Marshall Goldsmith, author of *Triggers: Creating Behavior that Lasts- Becoming the Person You Want to Be*, there are two immutable truths of behavioral change: 1) Meaningful behavioral change can be difficult to accomplish, and 2) No one can make an adult change against their will (2015). Behavioral change can be difficult to achieve as adults because we often reason our way into excuses that negate our need for change. There is a difference between motivation, understanding, and ability. Positive, consistent, behavioral change is challenging because we are attempting to change in an environment that is full of triggers (Goldsmith, 2015).

Those triggers may easily pull and push us off course. Fortunately, achieving meaningful and sustained change can be reached if we change what we believe (Goldsmith, 2015). The roots of what we believe is the driving force for our behavior. We must educate ourselves, and reinforce our critical thinking skills. We must question what we allow ourselves to believe, and allow our children see us in this process. Don't resist the need to change your behavior. There is always room for improvement.

I accept the challenge and opportunity to learn and grow daily. I am committed to being a better human being every day. I acknowledge, that although I am educated and compassionate to all people, the trauma that I have endured from many racist and discriminatory events in my life still effect what I say when I am in stressful situations.

We have to reject the notion that we do not need to grow and change. Although I am well read and have researched more on the topic of racism than most people I know, I still have plenty of room to grow and be compassionate to other people who are also in the process of growing. Often, it is easier to attack the strategy of the person who's trying to help than to try to solve the problem (Goldsmith, 2015). We as humans often fall back on a set of beliefs that trigger denial, resistance and ultimately self-delusion. They sabotage lasting change by canceling its possibility (Goldsmith, 2015). We employ these beliefs as articles of faith to justify our inaction and then wish away the result. These are called belief triggers.

This mentality of reconciliation of words and deeds will help us talk to our children about racism, live authentically and end racism in America. We must maintain our commitment to justice for all people, especially those who have been systematically oppressed as African Americans have. In our collective pursuit of prosperity and justice, I wholeheartedly wish you peace, power, and love.

REFERENCES

1. American Psychological Association. (2015 December 17). Retrieved from http://www.apa.org/about/gr/issues/health-care/disparities.aspx

2. Angelou, M., Neufeld, J.M. (January 16, 2011). *Oprah's Master Class.* Harpo Studios. Chicago, Il.

3. Brookfield, S.D. (2004). Critical thinking techniques. In M.W. Galbraith. *Adult learning methods: A guide for effective instruction.* (341-360). Malabar, Fl.

4. Buckley, T. R., & Carter, R. T. (2005). Black adolescent girls: Do gender role and racial identity impact their self-esteem? *Sex Roles.* (53) 647–666.

5. Coates, T. (2014, December 13). The case for reparations. *The Atlantic.* Retrieved from http://www.theatlantic.com/magazine/archive/2014/06/the-case-for-reparations/361631/

6. De Cremer, D., & Tyler, T. R. (2005). Managing group behavior: The interplay between procedural fairness, self, and cooperation. In M. Zanna (Ed.), *Advances in experimental social psychology.* (37) 152–218. New York, NY: Academic Press.

7. Evans, T. (1995). *Let's get to know each other.* Dallas, TX. Thomas Nelson Publishing Company.

8. Goldsmith, M. (2015). *Triggers: How to create behavior change that lasts.* New York, NY. Crown Publishing Group.

9. Gushue, G.V., Mejia-Smith, B. X., Fisher, L. D., Cogger, A., Gonzalez-Matthews, M., Lee, Y.J., Mancusi, L., McCullough, R., Connell, M. T., Weng, W.C., Cheng, M., Johnson, V. (2013). Differentiation of self and racial identity. *Counseling Psychology Quarterly.* 26 (3–4) 343–361.

10. Hale, W. (2015, December 24). Open-minded inquiry: Helping students assess their thinking. *The Critical Thinking Community.* Retrieved from http://www.criticalthinking.org/pages/open-minded-inquiry/579

11. Judt, T. (2005). Postwar: A History of Europe since 1945. London, England. Penguin Books, Ltd.

12. Lemley, K. (2014). Social justice in teacher education: Naming discrimination to promote transformative action. *Critical Questions in Education.* 5 (1) 26-51.

13. Morris, W. (2015, December 29). Some assumptions about power and rank in community art. Retrieved from http://www.wendymorris.org/resources/power_rank.pdf

14. Plante, T.G. (2013). How to spot a narcissist: Pretty easy when everywhere. *Psychology Today*. Retrieved from https://www.psychologytoday.com/blog/do-the-right-thing/201308/how-spot-narcissist-pretty-easy-when-everywhere

15. Thomas, C. (2015, December 30). Are you guilty of making hegemonic assumptions? *The Ethical Nag: Marketing Ethics for the Easily Swayed*. Retrieved from http://ethicalnag.org/2015/05/09/hegemonic-assumptions/

16. Developing critical thinking skills in children. (2015 December 30). Retrieved from http://www.brighthorizons.com/family-resources/e-family-news/2014-developing-critical-thinking-skills-in-children/

17. Whittemore, K. (2015, November 20). Raising a child who respects difference. *Parents Magazine*. Retrieved from http://www.parents.com/parenting/better-parenting/teaching-tolerance/raising-a-child-who-respects-difference/

18. Williams, M.T. (2015). The link between racism and PTSD: A psychologist explains race-based stress and trauma in Black Americans. *Psychology Today*. Retrieved from https://www.psychologytoday.com/blog/culturally-speaking/201509/the-link-between-racism-and-ptsd

19. Zerubavel, E. (1996). Social memories: Steps to a sociology of the past. *Qualitative Sociology*. 19 (3) 283-299.

20. Ziglar, Z. (2015 December 18). The answer to racism. *Creators.com*. Retrieved from http://www.creators.com/lifestylefeatures/inspiration/classic-zig-ziglar/the-answer-to-racism.html

ABOUT THE AUTHOR

Troya is regarded as a fierce fighter and advocate for social causes; with over 21 years of experience in advocacy and non-violent protests. She has extensive experience in long-term strategic planning, with various civil and human rights organizations.

Troya has been active in the social justice movement since attending NAACP meetings in Tuscaloosa, Alabama as a child. Tapped as a natural leader, she served in various leadership roles, as she continued to acquire more skills to become the best person, and leader possible. She served as a Leadership Commissioner (2010-2012) and Crisis Committee Chairperson in Rev. Al Sharpton's Atlanta office of National Action Network (2009-2012). Under the leadership of Rev. Sharpton, Troya was a key liaison in many cases regarding human rights violations. She was key in the mobilization effort to stop Troy Davis' execution by coordinating press campaigns, rallies, protests, and collaborating with many other organizations. She often speaks of the horror she felt and trauma she experienced after being at the prison with Troy's family and other activists when he was executed.

As a believer in the nonviolent approach to crisis resolution, she identifies closely with the philosophies of Dr. King and Mahatma Gandhi. Non-violent activism was a key approach to social change that she learned while earning her B.S. in Communications from Howard University. While completing her M.Ed. at Tennessee State University, her research was heavily comprised of (non-violent) strategies for working with children with behavior disorders. She is developing her skills to motivate and teach adults, as she earns her Doctorate of Education in Higher Education & Adult Learning from Walden University.

Other organizations that Troya is a member of are: The Southern Poverty Law Center, Amnesty International, Council for Exceptional Children, A.R.O.M.A, Georgians for the Alternatives to the Death Penalty (GFADP), Georgia Together and many other justice coalitions. Motivated by her commitment to teaching adults to advocate for themselves, Troya started her own non-profit organization, Parental Empowerment Institute (PEI), in October of 2012. Troya's passion for obtaining justice and equality for all and her ability to work with people earned her a permanent place in the movement, and a soft spot in the hearts of those she has served.

Purchase other Materials for your children & share your thouthts: theanswerstoracism.com
Twitter: @Answers2Racism and @OleBadd
Facebook: Facebook.com/TheAnswersAParentsGuide
Instagram: @OleBadd
Email: TheAnswers2@hotmail.com

COMING SOON!

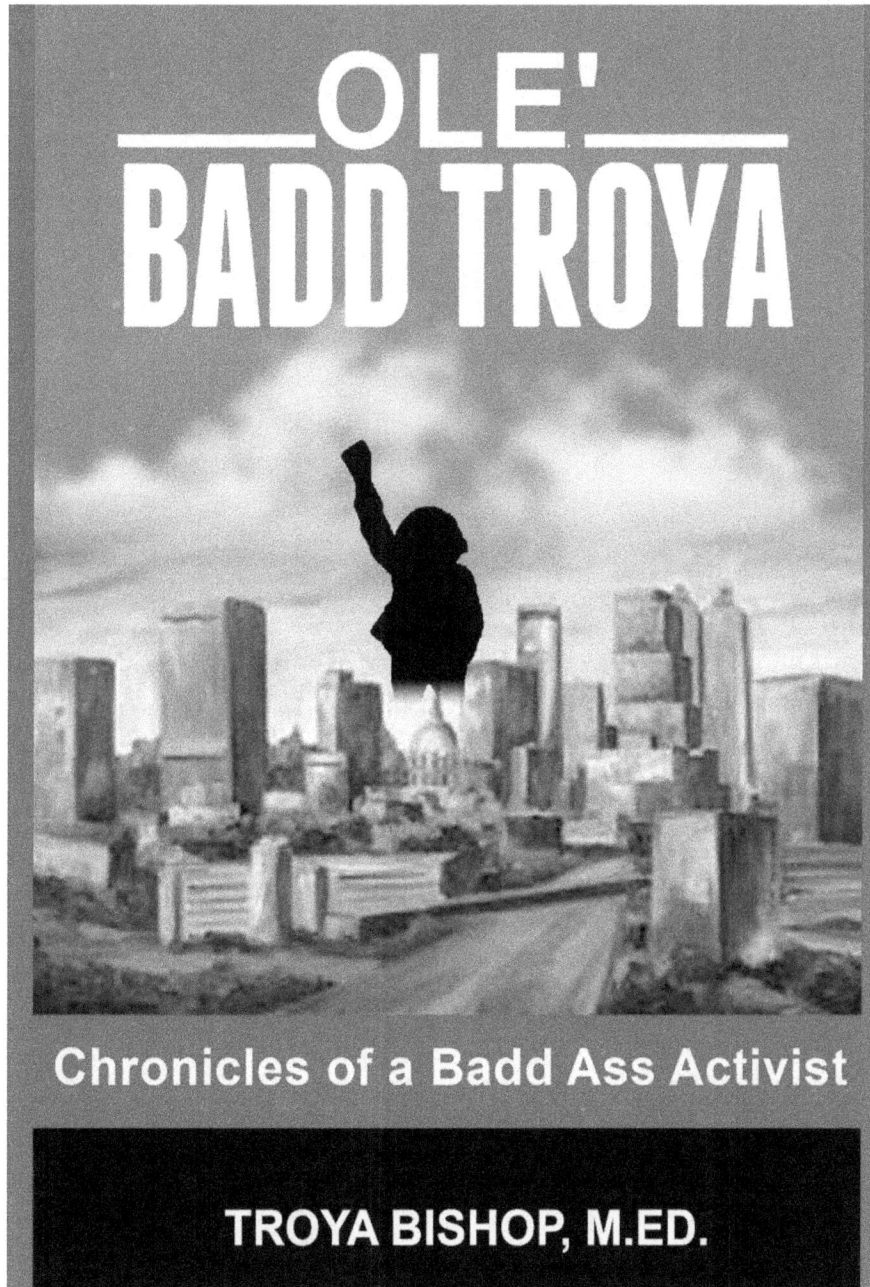

OLE'
BADD TROYA

Chronicles of a Badd Ass Activist

TROYA BISHOP, M.ED.

THANK YOU FOR YOUR SUPPORT